# Budget Bites

## 91 Ways To Cut Expenses And Conserve Cash

### MATTHEW JOHNSON

## DEDICATION

This book is dedicated to my Lord and Savior Jesus Christ who chose to allow difficult situations in my life so I could later use them for the good of others. It is also dedicated to my loving wife who has supported me and stood by my side as we struggled to make ends meet month after month. To my 4 beautiful children, you are the reasons I spend the time and energy searching for ways to save money. I pray that this book and investment of my time will pay dividends for generations to come. To my family, thanks for making me the person I am today. Dad thanks for teaching me how to find a good deal.

# CONTENTS

# INTRODUCTION

When my wife and I had our first child we went from living on two incomes to living on one. My job at the time did not provide enough money to make ends meet. I decided to start my own side business to supplement my income. Needless to say, my business idea failed miserably and left us $30,000 in debt. For the next ten years, we struggled to make it every month and keep from going bankrupt. We had to cut our monthly expenses out of pure necessity to survive. Today, we have four children and are still a single income family. We continue to look for creative ways to cut our expenses and save money. We have successfully utilized almost every budget bite in this book. We have now made it our goal to share these ideas and help others cut their own expenses and conserve some cash.

The Budget Bites book is setup for ease of use. It has fourteen different chapters listing specific areas where you can save money and create margin in your budget. There is also a final chapter that can help you create a financial plan that protects your family and assets, while allowing you to save money and get out of debt.

Each chapter will list some of the easiest and low cost ways to save money first. As the chapter progresses, the ideas become a little more time consuming or may require an upfront investment to set them in motion. Not everyone will utilize every idea in this book, nor will every idea apply to every person's situation. It has taken my wife and I thirteen years to accomplish everything talked about in this book. Please do not become overwhelmed by trying to accomplish everything overnight. My goal is to provide enough ideas that an average person or family could start saving enough money to change their financial situation within 30 days with little to no money out of their pocket.

Every money saving "bite" will have an empty box above it. The book is designed to be a user friendly reference guide for cutting your expenses and conserving cash. When you complete an idea, you can put a check mark in the box so you know it is done. If there is an idea that you would never use or does not apply to your situation, then you could put an "x" in the box. If it is an idea that you might come back to at a later date, then leave it blank.

My hope is that this book will help many people and families keep more of their hard earned cash. The goal is to create margin in your budget because margin ultimately equals less stress. I hope you enjoy using this book as much as I enjoyed writing it.

-MJ

# 1 ELECTRICITY

☐

The easiest way to save money on any utility bill is with an income based discount. Before you skip this section, thinking you make too much money, check out this example. In the state of California, where I live, a family of 5 can make up to almost $56,000 and still receive a twenty percent discount on their electric bill each month. If you make more than that, the same family of 5 can make up to almost $70,000 and receive another discount that lowers the price of the electricity in certain tiers.

These discounts are based on the number of people living in your house, not the number people you claim on your taxes. In California, a person with 8 people living in their house can make up to $100,000 a year and still receive the tier based discount. To find out if you qualify, call your local electric company or look on their website. There should also be a list of income guidelines and directions on how to sign up. This process is free and usually requires a minimal amount of time to process the application.

☐

Electric companies often offer incentives for you to save electricity. I live in a hot climate and I receive a $200 bill credit on my electricity bill every summer by participating in an A/C cycling program. The electric company put a box on my air conditioner and is able to turn it off for 30 minutes at a time during high demand days. My electric company also has "save power days" and I receive bill credits when I cut my usage on those days.

☐

Another way to save money is to install energy saving light bulbs (CFL or LED). These light bulbs use only a fraction of the electricity that a standard bulb would use. They can be rather expensive so look for incentives from your electric company. Sometimes they will offer them on their website or you will see the bulbs discounted in the store with an electric company "instant rebate."

☐

Every 6 months or so you should clean the dust off the coils under your refrigerator. This will allow it to perform at its best and save you electricity in the long run. It is also good to do this to a freezer and make sure it is defrosted at least once a year.

☐

A simple way to save electricity is to put power strips on all of your electronic devices. Electronic devices draw power even though they are not being used. A simple power strip allows you the ability to shut off the power to these devices when they are not in use. I often do this when my family and I go away on trips. I am also able to shut certain devices off at night.

☐

A family uses most of its electricity to cool or heat their house. Finding ways to limit the use of the air conditioner or forced heating unit will save a tremendous amount of money. During the summer months my family often uses the BBQ so we do not heat up the house with the oven. In the winter, we use the oven and it helps make the house warmer.

Below are a few more ideas that cost some money up front but will pay huge dividends in the long run.

☐

If you have power in your ceiling, a ceiling fan is a great way to save electricity. The fan will keep you cool during the summer months and then circulate the warm air in the winter months.

☐

If you live in an area that gets cool at night during the warmer months, a whole house fan is a great addition to your house. This large fan is installed in the attic in a central location of the house. The fan sucks air into the attic through self closing vents. When it is cool outside the fan is turned on and the windows of the house are opened. It draws the cool air inside and forces the hot air out of the attic. Some electric companies will even offer rebates if you install a whole house fan. These rebates can lower the initial cost of purchasing the fan and having it installed.

☐

If you live where the humidity is relatively low, an

evaporative cooler is a great investment. When my wife and I installed our evaporative cooler our electric bills where drastically reduced. Our bill went from $350 a month during the summer to under $100 a month. Many electric companies will also offer rebates for evaporative coolers if you get them ducted into your house. We chose to install a window mount cooler but there are many options available.

□

An electric area heater allows you to heat certain areas of your house and not have to heat the areas you are not using. They are often much cheaper than running your forced air heating unit. I also suggest closing ceiling vents and doors in rooms you are not using. This too can reduce the amount of time your heater or air conditioner has to run.

□

Older appliances use a lot of electricity. Many electric companies offer rebates to trade in old appliances and they have incentives to buy new "ENERGY STAR" appliances. Having a second refrigerator can be a contributing factor to a higher electric bill. Many people have an older model refrigerator outside or in their garage that is not energy efficient. Also, if you live in a hotter climate the refrigerator has to work a lot harder to keep the items cool. The same is true of freezers that are kept outside or in the garage. If you must have these appliances, try to put them somewhere cool.

□

A great way to save money is to generate your own electricity. The two most popular options are solar panels or a wind turbine. Both of these options take some careful planning and if purchasing, sometimes a large upfront investment. Many companies are now offering a solar lease or purchase program that requires zero out of pocket. In a solar lease, you are able to lock in the lower rate you will pay for electricity for 20+ years. The company leasing the equipment will usually maintain the system and will often install them for free. If you want an immediate savings, a lease may be a good option but purchasing the system could pay more dividends in the long run.

Going solar or installing a wind turbine can really increase your savings when combined with a plug in hybrid or electric car (see chapter 8). It can also save you money if you are able to switch to all electric appliances, electric area heaters, and a water heater. A person could virtually eliminate their gas or propane bill altogether.

☐

Some areas have special financing for many of the energy upgrades you might do to your house. In California where I live, we have the HERO (Home Energy Renovation Opportunity) program which allows a person to finance their energy upgrades and the payments are impounded as part of their property tax bill. There is a substantial tax benefit to this program which makes some of these bigger upgrades a little more affordable. *Energy.gov* has many resources to make your home more efficient and you can also search by state for rebates, programs, and low interest financing options. A simple Google search of your state or county may reveal other options available to you.

☐

Utility bills are often difficult to budget for because they often fluctuate. My family and I have taken advantage of our various utility company's level or equal payment plans. When you sign up for this program, your last 12 months of usage is added up, divided by 12, and that becomes your monthly bill. Therefore, you pay the same amount every month and there are no surprises. This makes the monthly budget process a lot more predictable.

If you are taking advantage of some of the money saving "bites" in this book, you may want to wait a few months before signing up for a level/equal payment. The utility companies re-average your yearly usage every 3 to 6 months so any savings made now will not show up for several months on a level/equal payment plan bill.

## 2 NATURAL GAS/PROPANE

☐

As with any utility, the easiest way to save money is to determine if you qualify for an income based discount. As I stated in the electricity chapter, there are certain income guidelines that must be met. However, most people do not think they qualify when they actually do. The guidelines are usually universal among utility companies in the same geographic area. Ultimately, if you qualify for one, you will usually qualify for all of them.

When I still met the income guidelines, my family received a 20 percent discount on our electric and natural gas bill as well as a discount on our water bill. Depending on your usage and size of home, these discounts can add up quickly and result in hundreds of dollars in savings. To find out if you qualify, simply call your utility company or visit their website to view their special programs.

☐

If you have a gas/propane water heater, it can drive up

your gas/propane bill. A simple way to save money is to turn down the temperature on the water heater. In many instances, the water temperature at a person's home is hotter than it needs to be. This in turn uses more gas/propane to keep the water at that temperature.

☐

For around $30 you can purchase a water heater blanket. This insulating device will improve the energy efficiency of your water heater by keeping the heat in and the cold out. These can be found at your local hardware store or online at *amazon.com*.

☐

Recapturing heat during the winter can help save on your gas or propane bill. Using the oven to cook will help heat the house as the heat escapes from it. You can also leave the door open to your laundry room while drying clothes to allow that heat into the rest of the house. Although these appliances help warm the house, they should never be used as a primary source of heat as there is a risk of carbon monoxide poisoning.

☐

A simple way to save money on your gas/propane bill is change the way you do laundry. Washing most of your laundry with cold water will limit the amount of hot water you use and save you money. Also, if you are able to use a clothesline or drying rack to dry your clothes, this will also cut down on your gas/propane bill if you have a dryer that runs on gas/propane.

☐

Another way to save money in the area of heating

water is to limit the amount of hot water used. In the water chapter I discuss the use of low flow shower heads and water saving appliances that can help you accomplish this.

☐

As I stated before, the use of area heaters can save money over heating the entire house. Not only does this save money on your electric bill it will also cut down your gas/propane bill. If a person has a solar system or wind turbine, the use of electric area heaters can be extremely beneficial.

☐

More and more people have switched to a tankless water heater. These water heaters save money on your gas/propane bill by only heating water when it is needed instead of keeping a large amount of water hot all the time. I have not personally used a tankless water heater but my friends have had mixed reviews on the temperature of the water. Make sure you do your research and get one that has good reviews unless you like lukewarm showers.

☐

If your house is equipped with a fireplace, adding an insert and a wood burning stove can save a considerable amount of money on your gas/propane bill. Before considering this option, check to see if your geographic area has "burn" and "no burn days." I know several people who live in areas of high pollution and this becomes an issue. They are not allowed to use their fireplaces or wood burning stoves as much as they would like due to "no burn days." You would not want to invest the money into a wood burning stove and then find out you could not use it.

You should also check the costs of firewood in your area. If firewood or pellets are expensive, then a natural gas/propane heater may be a better option.

☐

Your local natural gas/propane company may also offer incentives or programs to increase the energy efficiency of your home, thus saving you money on your bill. Sometimes these programs require income qualification or the homeowner to spend money for the repairs. Call or visit their website to see what is available in your area.

## 3 WATER

☐

Your water bill, much like you gas and electric bill, may qualify for and income based rate reduction. This information is available by calling or checking your local water company's website.

☐

A lot of water and money is wasted in the bathroom. An easy way to save money in the bathroom is to install low flow shower heads. One option is to purchase new shower heads that are low flow and limit the amount of gallons per minute that pass through them. This may cost a little more money but these shower heads are designed to work with a low flow of water. We use the Niagara Earth Massage 1.25 gallon per minute low flow shower head. It is available on *amazon.com* for under $10 and still provides great water flow. A cheaper route would be to buy a water restrictor that is placed inside the shower head. These restrictors limit the amount of water passing through the shower head but may also affect the performance of the shower head if it is not designed for low water flow. If you want to save money on your water bill you should try to do one or the other.

□

There are many water saving toilets on the market but they are often costly. There are some simple tricks to make your current toilet more efficient without having to spend the money on a new one. There are a variety of different two stage flush conversions for your toilet. These devices make it possible to get a half flush for small jobs and a full flush for large jobs. If you are looking to spend even less money, *instructables.com* offers a how to article so you can convert your current toilet to be a water saver. With minor adjustments, your toilet will only flush halfway by pushing down the handle and flush all the way when you hold down the handle.

□

*Amazon.com* also sells water displacement bladder bags for the toilet. These bags are filled with water and hung on the inside of the toilet tank. Every time the toilet is flushed, the amount of water inside the bladder bag is saved. Niagara also makes a bladder like this that we use in our home called "the toilet tank bank."

□

A simple adapter on the end of your bathroom faucets can limit the water flow down to as little as one half gallon per minute. This device is called a water saving aerator and is available online and at most hardware stores. They are inexpensive and an easy way to save water and money. They are also sold for kitchen faucets as well. Once again, we use the Niagara half gallon per minute faucet aerators that we purchased on *amazon.com*.

☐

The next place a lot of water is wasted is on landscaping. Some water companies have a "cash for grass" program. This program pays the homeowner a certain amount of money per square foot to change from grass to some form of drought or low water landscaping. Most water companies will have this information on their website or it is available by calling. If you can live without grass and you live in a warm climate this program can help you cut your water bill drastically.

☐

I have been able to save water by changing the times of day that I water my lawn. I use to water my lawn three times a day due to the fact I live in a hot climate. I changed to twice a day by watering once at about 4am and again at 10 or 11am. By doing this, I was able to cut one whole cycle of watering out and my grass is just as green.

☐

Another way to save a little water is to have a bucket in your showers to catch the water while you wait for it to become warm. This water can be used to water outdoor and indoor plants. A 5 gallon painter bucket works well and can be picked up at any hardware store for under $5.

☐

Rain barrels are a great way to water outdoor landscaping. These barrels catch the rain runoff from your gutters and the water can be used to water plants later on. Many of them hold 50+ gallons of water and have hose attachment on the bottom. Rain barrels are illegal in some areas so check with the local municipalities before purchasing one for your home.

□

The use of water saving appliances to wash your dishes and clothes also saves water. When it is time to buy a new dishwasher, buy one with a hard food disposer built in. This limits the need for any pre rinsing and saves a lot of water. Dishwashers are always more efficient than washing dishes by hand even with an aerator on the kitchen faucet.

# 4 TRASH

You are probably thinking, how can I possibly save money on my trash bill?  The answer is very simple, trash companies usually charge you based on the amount of trash you have. Many of these companies do not advertise it, but they have separate charges based on the size trash can you have or how many times they pick up.

□

When I set up my service, I was given a large trash can and recycle can.  It was not until later on that I realized there were 3 different size cans and I had the largest.  I called my trash company and ordered a medium size can which saved me $5 a month.  $5 a month doesn't seem like much but when combined with several of the other discounts in this book, it really begins to add up.  The trash company also told me I could have more than one recycle can for free.  My wife and I started separating out the recyclables and we were able to save a lot of room in the regular trash can.  There are months where we have more trash than our can allows but we have our own trash can to store the trash in if need be. To take advantage of this "budget bite", simply call your trash company and ask if they have different size cans and rates.

# 5 TV, PHONE, INTERNET

I listed these three items in one chapter because they are typically bundled together on one bill . Most people are overpaying for one if not all of these services. There are always ways to save on these services and below I list several that have worked for me and my family.

☐

Most companies will start you with a discounted bundle rate to lock you in to a 12-24 month contract. Once this contract expires, your bill reverts to the standard price and you start overpaying for these services. A person has two options, switch providers every two years or get your current provider to lower their rate. I have switched providers several times but it is not always cost effective. Many times you are charged set up and activation fees that may eat up any of the savings you would have received over the course of a year.

If you like your current service, your provider will do a lot to keep you from leaving. I usually find a competitors rate and call in to see if they will match it. Most of the time the operator will offer some sort of discount for 12 months or try to get you to sign a new contract. Your biggest discount usually comes when you tell them you want to cancel your service. Often you are transferred to a department whose sole job is to keep you from quitting their service. These agents have much more flexibility in what they can offer you as far as discounts go. There is some room for negotiation so do not think you have to accept their first offer.

□

If you do decide to cancel your service, you might not want to sign a contract with your new provider right away. Usually a few months after you cancel your service with a provider, you will receive some highly discounted offers from them in the mail. The last time I changed providers, the lowest my old provider would go was $89.99 a month for a new 24 month contract. Two months later, I received an offer from my old provider in the mail for $59.99 a month for the same services. Once again, make sure you watch the activation and cancelation fees so you do not end up paying more than you are saving in the long run.

□

Another easy way to save some money is to get rid of your land telephone line. A lot of people have done this and choose to use a cell phone instead. Some people have kept their land line so they will have service if the cell towers go down. What they do not know is that most phone providers have switched to a "Voice over Internet Protocol" (VoIP) service. Due to the fact the internet in your home relies on electricity to work, your phone will stop working if the power goes out. Often there is a battery back up on the system but that usually only lasts 30 minutes.

I called my provider and I was told because I had fiber optic service, I could no longer get the traditional land line (which was a much cheaper option). If you do not have a cell phone or want to have a separate line for the house, Magic Jack, or service like it, is a much cheaper option to traditional phone service. Magic Jack is a small device you plug into your personal computer that allows you to make calls over the internet.

☐

My family recently stopped paying for television altogether to save money. We did not watch a lot of the channels and to be frank we were disgusted by most of the commercials that came on between shows. We were constantly telling our young children to look away during commercials while we were watching a family friendly show.

We chose to get an Apple TV box. There are many different devices (Fire TV, Roku, Chromecast, etc.) that can do many of the same things as Apple TV. Apple TV can be a bit pricey so we went to the Apple Store online and bought a refurbished model. This saved us about $20 off the retail price of the box.

Apple TV is continually adding new channels and if you have an iPad, iPhone, or new iPod you can "Air Play" videos and channels from those devices to your TV. Most of the Disney owned channels (currently ABC, ESPN channels, and 3 Disney channels) are available on Apple TV. You can also use Netflix or Hulu to stream shows on your box. Most networks have an app that allows you to watch most of your popular shows (some require a login) or you can now pay for certain channels "a la carte." To be honest, my family has not missed regular television and neither has my wallet.

□

There are several internet television services that are available and often cost less than traditional television service. Unlike traditional streaming services, you are able to watch live television with these services. They are a great way to watch television for those who are afraid to cut the cable completely. One of the most popular services on the market right now is Sling and it only costs about $20 a month. The service includes channels like ESPN, Disney, TNT, A&E, etc.

□

"Over the Air" channels are another way to save money on TV and can be used in conjunction with Apple TV, Fire TV, Roku, or Chromecast. *Antennaweb.org* is a great resource to see if there are channels in your area that can be picked up using an antenna. There is an upfront investment to get the antenna but these are free high definition channels that you will get for years to come. These channels often include ABC, CBS, NBC, FOX, and KCET. I purchased an amplified antenna from *amazon.com* for $30 and it sits on my back porch. It was easy to set up and is rather small. There are plenty of antenna models that do not have to be mounted on your roof. I am able to watch most of the major networks and several other local channels at no cost to me per month.

If you are able to eliminate TV and your telephone landline the only thing left to pay for is your internet service that will support your TV box, VoIP telephone service, and internet enabled devices. This chapter alone has the potential to save you over $100 a month if you are willing to part with the traditional service. I firmly believe that eventually all TV will be streamed over the internet so we might as well save some money with it while we can.

# 6 CELL PHONE

15 years ago, not too many people had a line item in their budget for a cell phone. Now with smart phones, texting, and families having multiple lines, the cost to have a cell phone plan has gone up dramatically. Below are a few ways to save on your cell phone bill so it does not take such a huge chunk out of your budget every month.

☐

Almost all cell phone companies offer discounts for different professional organizations. As an educator, I receive a 15% discount on my total bill. The best way to find out if you qualify is to call your provider or visit their website for their list of occupations, unions, and organizations that receive a discount. If you do not qualify, there are often many organizations you can join for little to no cost that will allow you to receive a discount on your bill.

☐

Most cell phone companies are now offering "bring your own device" plans that offer discounted rates on the service. If you purchase your own phone, or already have one, this is a great way to save on your monthly bill and not be locked into a contract. I personally have T-Mobile because they have offered me the lowest rates and I receive a 15% discount as an educator. I have five phones and pay just over $100 a month with all my taxes and fees included. The data speed slows down after 1gb of data per line but 1gb is more than I ever use per phone.

☐

Another benefit to T-Mobile is that they offer wifi calling. I work in a building that seems to interfere with cell phone signals. Most of my coworkers have to go outside to make a call. When my T-Mobile phone is connected to the wifi, I am able to send and receive calls as well as text messages over the internet. I never have to miss my calls or texts anymore.

Wifi calling can also save a lot of money if you travel outside the country or if you are out of cell signal range. As long as you make your calls over wifi, you are not charged roaming or airtime fees. Wifi is obviously showing up in more and more places like airplanes, cruise ships, busses, etc. and that makes my T-Mobile phone useful in all those places, even if there is no cell service.

My family recently went camping in the mountains well out of cell signal range. The campground had wifi that we paid for and I was able to send and receive all of my calls and text messages.

☐

With the "bring your own device" plans it is often cheaper to buy a "pay as you go" phone and have it activated on your monthly plan than to buy a phone in your provider's store(check with your provider first to make sure they allow you to activate a "pay as you go" phone on your monthly plan). My wife lost her phone and we were able to get her a new Nokia phone for about $70 on sale at Target (the same phone at the my providers store was $130). Not only was the phone on sale but I received 5% off with my Target RedCard.

# 7 GROCERIES

There are entire websites that are set up for extreme couponing and ways to save on your grocery bill. I do not intend to go into that amount of detail in this book. However, I do want to share how my wife and I save money every month without having to spend a lot of time and energy to be an extreme couponer.

□

We do a lot of shopping at Target and we maximize our discounts wherever we can. Not everyone has a Target or SuperTarget nearby, but if you do this information could save you a lot of money.

If you shop at Target and you are not using their RedCard, you are leaving money on the table. Their RedCard allows you to save 5% on all of your purchases and receive free shipping when you purchase online. If you do not like credit cards, they have a RedCard debit option that comes right out of your checking account and you still receive the discounts and benefits.

If you were to buy all of your groceries and toiletries at Target and spend $1000 in a month, you would automatically save $50 just by using the RedCard.

☐

Target allows you to coupon stack. If you go to Target.com you can print their store coupons and you will usually receive coupons from the register when you check out. You can also sign up for mobile coupons that will be text to you. The nice thing is you can also use a manufacture coupon for the same item and stack on the savings.

☐

My wife and I also use Target's Cartwheel app which allows you to pick several items and receive extra percent off discounts. These discounts are usually an additional 5-50% off and are added to the RedCard 5%. By stacking these savings, we often receive 10-15% off of the items we purchase most (not including the coupons we use). The more you use the Cartwheel app, the more discounts they allow you to use during a purchase. The first year my wife and I used Cartwheel we saved about $100 but that amount has increased substantially over time.

☐

Target also has a pharmacy rewards program for refilling prescriptions with your RedCard. After five prescriptions, you will received a 5% discount certificate in the mail to use on a purchase. We usually save this discount certificate until we make a big shopping trip at the beginning of the month. This 5% certificate is added to the Cartwheel discounts and the 5% for using your RedCard.

By combining all the Target offers and coupons we

are able to save well over $100 a month on our grocery and toiletry bill. Some of it takes a little planning but it is money easily saved.

◻

My wife and I shop at conventional grocery stores as well and when we do, we try to maximize our saving by using a cash reward credit card. We currently have a reward credit card that pays us 6% cash back on groceries, 3% back on fuel and select department stores and 1% on everything else.

As with any credit card, you are only going to save money if you are disciplined enough to pay it off each month. Paying interest on your grocery and fuel bill will not save you money.

My wife and I had to do some research but we found the right card for us. It did have a $70 annual fee which I am not a fan of but we got a $100 bonus for signing up which paid for the annual fee the first year. The percentages we get back are so much higher than any other card, we are quickly able to pay for the subsequent annual fees and still get cash back

If you were to spend $800 on groceries and $400 on fuel in a month, you would receive $60 cash back that month. When you multiply that by 12 months and subtract out the $70 annual fee, that is $650 cash back you would earn annually or about $54 a month. Obviously, if you spend more or less these numbers will change.

◻

Many grocery store chains release their ads on Wednesdays and this is usually the best day to shop because the deals are almost guaranteed to be there on the first day. Some grocery chains are allowing customers to shop two ads on the same day (last week's ad and the coming week's ad) and this is another reason to shop the day the ad comes out.

□

Coupons will always save you money as well as using store discount cards. There are plenty of online coupon sites if you do not receive coupons in the Sunday paper. Also, make sure you save the coupons that print out at the register when you check out. Many of these coupons print based on items you have purchased previously. You can sometimes buy certain coupons on eBay for different retailers that can save you a lot of money when you are making a large purchase. For example $8 for a 10% off coupon is a good deal if you have to make a $500 purchase. That is a savings of $42.

□

My wife and I have shopped at grocery stores that also have a fuel reward option as well. 10-15 cents off 30 gallons of fuel saves us an extra $3-$4 at the pump. Obviously, if the gas costs more than you would pay somewhere else, then it is almost pointless to utilize this option.

□

Another simple way to save some money is to bring your own reusable bags to the store. Many stores like Target and others will give you five cents per reusable bag that you bring and use. Every twenty bags you bring will be another dollar in your pocket. It may not seem like much but as I have stated before, little bits add up at the end of the month. These little lifestyle changes become habits and reap big rewards over the course of a year.

☐

Buying items in bulk can often save a chunk of money if done properly.  My wife and I like to shop at Costco for our bulk items and it saves us a lot of money with 4 growing kids.  Most bulk item stores charge a membership fee and this is where they make a lot of their money.  We take advantage of Costco's Executive Membership that gives us 2% back on what we spend.  The reward we earn each year usually covers the cost of our Executive Membership, thus making it even cheaper to shop there.

☐

The USDA has drawn up a "thrifty food plan" and put it on their website as a resource for families to use.  It is a meal plan to help a family eat healthy and save money.  They usually update the average food costs every month.  *Cheapism.com* often puts together healthy meal planning ideas on their website.  At the time I wrote this chapter, there was an article called "How to live on $500 a month at Costco."  It detailed how to feed a family of 4 by shopping at Costco for only $500 a month.  There are many other resources out there like this to help trim the costs of an ever rising grocery budget.

## 8 FUEL

Saving money on fuel for your vehicle is always a popular topic due to the price increases we have seen over the last decade. I will share a few easy ideas and some that require more thought and planning. All of these ideas have saved my family a lot of money over the years.

□

One of the easiest ways to save on fuel is to make sure your vehicle is properly maintained. Keeping your tires properly inflated is very important when it comes to saving fuel. Underinflated tires create more roll resistance and use more fuel. Most tires have a higher maximum pressure than your vehicle recommended pressure. Extra air pressure in your tires may give you a stiffer ride but it will save a little more on fuel. As with anything of this nature, please check with your mechanic before changing anything on your car.

□

Synthetic Oil can be a money saving tool. It allows you

to go further between oil changes and creates less friction in the engine which can ultimately save on fuel mileage costs. Synthetic oil costs more but if you change it less the initial cost balances out.

☐

Cash back credit cards are an easy way to save money on fuel. As I stated in the previous chapter, my wife and I use a cash back card that gives us 3% back on all of our fuel purchases. If you were using this card and spent $500 a month on fuel, then you would earn $15 cash back. If you shop at a grocery store that gives a fuel discount with your grocery purchases, then you could easily save $25 or more every month on fuel costs.

☐

Hypermiling is another way to save money on fuel. If you Google the term hypermiling, you will find many examples and definitions associated with the idea. You may find many ideas that are not safe like going around corners at 50+mph or taking off your side view mirrors to reduce drag. However, I have found many ideas that a person can use to improve their fuel economy without being extreme or dangerous. When you read some of the articles, you will be amazed at how many things you do while driving that wastes fuel.

☐

Extra weight in your car always reduces your fuel economy. The EPA has said that every extra 100 pounds of weight in your vehicle will result in a 2% loss in fuel economy. This is why many new cars do not have a spare tire anymore. Make sure you are not toting around extra weight in your trunk, bed, or back seats.

☐

A simple way to save money on fuel is to have someone else pay for it. You can do this by turning your car into a mobile billboard. There are companies out there willing to pay you every month to put advertisements on your car. Make sure you do your research because there are also a lot of scams. I personally have had the privilege of working with a company called AdverCar. I participated in one of their marketing campaigns and received $100 a month just for driving back and forth to work with vinyl stickers on the sides of my car. If you meet the qualifications, it is an easy way to cut your fuel expenses each month.

☐

Alternative fuel vehicles are a great way to save on fuel if they fit your circumstances and lifestyle. My wife and I have owned two CNG (compressed natural gas) vehicles and I currently drive an EV (electric vehicle). Both have saved us money and they are not as expensive as they might seem.

When gas first went up to $4 a gallon I knew my tight budget could not absorb that cost. I decided to sell my current vehicles and change over to compressed natural gas (CNG). I bought two vehicles that happened to be bi-fuel, meaning they can run on CNG or gasoline. Depending on where you live in the country, CNG prices can be much cheaper than gasoline or diesel. *CNGprices.com* has a map where you can determine the price of natural gas in your area.

Many large metropolitan areas have taxis, vans, and busses that run on CNG. You will usually see a blue diamond on the back with the letters CNG in it. Most of these cities have fueling stations that are usually open to the public. Where I live, the CNG price is about a dollar cheaper for a gas gallon equivalent of CNG than for a gallon of gasoline or diesel. It is not uncommon in many areas for it to be two dollars or more cheaper

Dedicated CNG vehicles and bi-fuel vehicles each have their positives and negatives. Honda makes a Civic that is dedicated CNG and also sells a home fueling station that could potentially make the price of refueling even cheaper. Many of the used CNG vehicles were former government vehicles and can be found at auctions, CNG vehicle dealers, or used car websites (key words "alternative fuel vehicles"). I could probably write an entire book on this topic but I will try to keep it short and say, make sure you do your research. If done properly this can save you a lot of money on fuel.

□

The latest rage is Electric Vehicles or EV's. I currently own the all electric Nissan Leaf and love it. The overall range is about 85 miles. This car is not for everyone and should not be the only car you own. I commute about 38 miles round trip to work every day so it works well for me. The Leaf is rated at 118mpge which means it will go 118 miles on what it would cost to buy one gallon of gas. Ultimately, it is like having a car that gets 118 miles per gallon of gas.

I was intrigued by electric cars when they first came out but I did not buy one. It never made sense to pay $40,000 for a car to save money on fuel when I could get a fuel efficient car for $16,000. I could buy a lot of fuel with $24,000. Car companies are under pressure by the federal government to sell more of these vehicles to meet fuel mileage and environment requirements so the costs have been coming down (especially if you lease the vehicle).

The government offers a $7,500 tax credit off the price of an Electric Vehicle. You pay this money up front and file for the credit on your taxes if you are purchasing the vehicle. However, if you lease the vehicle, like I did, the car company files for the credit and you get it off the price of the car immediately. I also put $3,000 down to lower my payment and I received $2,500 cash back from my state in the form of a credit. My Leaf started out at $32,000 but was reduced $10,000 by the state and federal credits. I was able to do some haggling and my lease payment is under $200 a month

When I bought my EV I also installed an evaporative cooler on my house at the same time. My electric bill actually went down even though I started charging my car at home. By combining these two things I ultimately eliminated my $160-$200 a month gasoline bill and was still able to lower my electricity bill. My next step is to possibly upgrade to solar and save even more money.

The incentives for electric vehicles continue to get better and their range continues to grow as the battery technology improves. Some companies are now offering free charging on several different nationwide networks a year or two after you buy the car. This will save you even more money if you do not have to pay for all of the electricity.

## 9 RECYCLING

Recycling is not an expense but the money you gain from it can be used to create some margin and extra income at times you may need it most.

☐

My family recycles our empty water bottles and soda cans to help us earn some extra money. Every 2-3 months, we earn $20-$30 for collecting and turning them in. In many states, every time you buy something in a bottle or can, you are charged a redemption value or deposit at the time of purchase. By recycling, you are cutting down the amount of money you pay for anything that comes in a bottle or can. If you do not recycle, you are actually increasing the amount of money you pay in tax every month. There are often coupons in the newspaper that increase the price you receive per pound on your recycled items. My wife and I often use the money we receive from our bottles and cans to do fun things with our kids. This is an easy way to take them out when we do not have the extra money in our budget to do so. This reward system also gets our kids excited about recycling. They in turn got their grandparents involved and started asking them for their bottles and cans as well.

□

If you are not a person who refills your ink or toner cartridges to save money, then there are many office supply stores that will recycle your old ink and toner cartridges. Most of these stores will give you $3-$4 per cartridge in the form of rewards or store credits. This could save you money on the purchase of your new toner, ink cartridge, or other office supplies.

□

If you search around your house, there are many different metals and items that can be recycled if you need some quick money. My wife and I have sold our broken or unused gold and silver and received money that same day. These items have included, broken chains, anklets, bent rings, etc. Most gold buying companies will even buy the gold off of a capped tooth that a person has lost. Many people do not realize there is often hundreds of dollars sitting around your house that could be turned into quick cash.

## 10 INSURANCE

I am sure entire books are written on this topic. I am going to be brief and hit a few key ways to save some money on something we all have to pay for on a monthly basis.

□

Auto Insurance: Every auto insurance company says they can save you money but that is not always the case. Make sure you shop around to find the best rates and the coverage you need. Like the cell phone companies, many insurance companies will give you a discount based on your profession. As an educator, I am able to save a lot of money. Call your insurance company or check their website to find the list of professions that receive a discount.

□

If you decrease the amount of miles you drive in a year, make sure you update this with your insurance company.  The more miles you drive, the more you will pay for insurance.  Some insurance companies are now offering discounts if you drive an alternative fuel vehicle as well.

☐

Life Insurance:  Back in the 70's and 80's there was a company called A.L. Williams that championed the phrase, "buy term and invest the difference."  The idea is to buy term life insurance instead of any type of life insurance with a savings/cash back option.  Term insurance is much cheaper and  a person can invest the money saved to get a greater return.  With term insurance, you can lock in a low rate for 10, 20, or 30+ years.  Life insurance should be used to protect your family while you are building wealth for retirement.  It should not be something you pay for your whole life.

Most life insurance companies have term options but you will have to shop around for the best price.  The agents will make the other options sound attractive because they often do not make as much commission on term life insurance. Sometimes you will have to be adamant if you want term insurance.  Try to find a policy that will cover you and your family until at least retirement.

Beware of accidental death and dismemberment insurance policies.  They are very cheap and often only pay when very strict accidental death criteria are met.  Some of these policies will not pay unless you die in the accident immediately.  If you are in an accident and later die at the hospital, your death is no longer considered an accident.

☐

Home Owners Insurance:  An easy way to save on your home owners insurance policy is to bundle it with your auto insurance.  However, make sure you shop around because bundling may not always be the best deal. I have had my home and auto insurance separate and was able to save more money this way. Certain things like the type of dog you own, if you have a pool, and if you have a trampoline can also cause your rates to go up dramatically.

□

Health Insurance: There are many ways to save on health insurance. If you have a private policy outside of work, make sure you shop around often. Many companies will offer a lower rate to get you to switch but will raise your rate as time progresses. If you are a person that rarely has any major medical issues, you might consider a plan that has a higher deductible. These plans usually have a lower monthly cost but will cost you more money when they are used. Another way to save is to take advantage of a Health Savings Account if it is available to you. Money put into this account goes in pre-tax but can only be used for medical expenses. This account will help reduce the amount of money you pay in taxes each year. However, it is a bit of a gamble at times because you lose any unused money at the end of the year.

## 11 TAXES

A good CPA or tax advisor can often show you many different ways to save money by paying less in income taxes. That is not my goal in this chapter, I will leave that to the professionals. I want to talk about your tax refund.

☐

Tax refunds are always nice and many people often rely on them every year to pay off bills, take a vacation, or some other big expenditure. If your tax refund is something you rely on every year, then this chapter may not be for you.

Any refund you receive is money that you loaned the government during the year (interest free). This book is all about putting your hard earned money back in pocket so here is what I did with my tax refund.

I used an app from Turbo Tax called "TaxCaster." This simple app allows you to put in your basic financials and estimate the amount of income tax you will pay. Your CPA or tax advisor should be able to do the same thing and in more detail if needed. Once you know the amount of tax you need to pay, then you can look at adjusting your exemptions to reduce the amount of tax coming out of your paycheck each month. I adjusted my exemptions so I still receive about $500-$800 in refund each year. I leave some buffer because no one likes to have to pay taxes at the end of the year.

I have heard that the average American receives roughly $3,000 back in taxes every year. If a person in this situation adjusted their exemptions to where their refund was only $600 instead of $3000 then they would receive $200 more a month on their paycheck. I don't know about you, but $200 more a month is a lot of money when living on a tight budget.

Obviously, you would not have the large chunk of money you once had during refund time but the $200 a month could really help a person or family manage their budget each month and stay out of debt. Make sure you consult your CPA or tax advisor before making changes to your tax situation.

# 12 GIFT AND REWARD CARDS

We live in an era where gift cards have replaced traditional gifts at Christmas, birthdays, and life events. Almost everyone has received a gift card they really did not want and almost everyone has used a gift card to make a major purchase. To capitalize on these two things I have found there are websites out there that allow you to buy and sell discounted gift cards.

☐

If you receive a gift card you do not want, you can sell it at a discounted rate to a card exchange website. The reputable sites will send you money for your unused gift cards (make sure you research the website before doing business with them). You will not receive the full value of the card but it is a simple way to put some money in your pocket. Most of these sites list the rates upfront so you can calculate how much you will receive before you sell your gift card to them. You can also sell your gift card on eBay but it could end up costing you more in fees when it is all said and done.

□

You can also use card exchange websites to save money when you are purchasing items. You can buy gift cards on these sites at a discounted rate. For instance, the card may have a $100 value but is sold for $90 at a 10% discount. By using the gift card, you are saving the percentage discount on whatever you buy. I like to use *giftcardgranny.com* because it lists multiple discount rates for the gift card you are looking for from many different card exchange websites, including eBay.

Buying discounted gift cards is a great way to save money on going out to dinner, the movies, shopping, and major purchases. For example, my wife and I decided to get new carpet for our house. We purchased the carpet through a major home improvement retailer during their free installation sale. The total cost to carpet our house was $6,500 with the free installation. We negotiated with the salesperson on the price and he discounted our cost down to $6,300. We were able to get a 10% off coupon for the store on eBay for $3. This coupon was only good for the price of the carpet and not the pad so it discounted the price down $460 to $5,840. We then bought gift cards online for the price of the carpet. The discount on the gift cards at the time was 9.4% of the value of the gift card. The total cost of the gift cards were just under $5,300. We bought the gift cards with a cash back credit card and we earned $53 dollar back on the purchase. The final cost for our carpet was about $5,240 compared to the original $6500. By combining a coupon, discounted gift cards, cash back credit card and negotiating the price we were able to save $1,260 on the price of our carpet. With the money we saved we were able to do several other home improvement projects as well.

□

If you are a person who likes to give gift cards, gift card exchange websites are another way to save money on gift shopping. There are numerous stores, movie houses, and food establishments available at discounted rates and usually the shipping is free.

□

Most stores now have some sort of reward card that helps you save money. Even though I know they are collecting information on me, I am a proponent of using these cards to get as much money back as you can. For some grocery stores it means 10-30 cents off a gallon of gasoline or discounts on product. At department stores, it may mean cash back or extra percent off discounts. Utilize it all to your advantage.

□

Many major retailers, hardware stores and gas stations often have their own credit card that offers some sort of perk when you use it. It may be a discount off your purchase when you sign up, rewards for every dollar spent or a gift card to the store once you have purchased a certain dollar amount. In any of these options, there are ways to leverage these cards to your advantage. However, if you are not disciplined enough to spend within your means and to pay the card off at the end of the month, then you are not saving money. You end up paying more in interest than you would ever save. My wife and I try to use these perks when we have a major purchase to make. We have been able to save on large home improvement purchases, receive an instant credits online and reduce the amount of money we spend at the holidays. If you have good credit and are disciplined in your spending there are many ways to save on a lot of the things you have to buy.

# 13 TRAVEL/VACATION

Whether you have to travel for business or pleasure we have found several ways to cut costs and even vacation for free. Everyone wants to take a vacation with their family or with a significant other and these are some simple ways to make it affordable even for the tightest budget.

☐

Every major hotel chain, airline, and cruise line usually has some type of credit card that offers an incentive if you sign up and spend a certain dollar amount in the opening months of card ownership. My wife and I have often used these free rewards to our advantage when we are going on vacation. Many people do not realize that each family member over 18 can sign up for their own credit card and get the promotional reward. For instance, my wife and I signed up for a hotel chains credit card and received 40,000 bonus points each. That was enough points to stay in a nice room for almost a week for free. Free rooms, flights, and discounted cruises can be easily attained if you have good credit and can be disciplined in your spending.

☐

Whether you are a novice or a pro when it comes to reward credit cards, there is a website that will give you a wealth of information for earning free rewards and discounted trips. *Onemileatatime.com* offers simple guides to get started as well as links to reward programs and credit cards. Their sister site, *pointspros.com* can help you book your vacation with your points and miles and get the most out of every reward point or dollar you have earned. Another great website for finding ways to use reward cards is *millionmilesecrets.com*.

☐

If you travel for work or business, make sure you sign up for your hotel, airline, and rental car rewards programs. Even though you travel to conferences, meetings, and engagements that are paid for by your employer, you are still able to collect the points you earn on your rooms, flights and rental cars. You can in turn use those points for free rooms, flights, and rental cars during your personal vacations.

☐

Timeshare presentations are an easy way to save money on vacationing. By attending a timeshare presentation you can earn free nights at a resort, free tickets to shows, and even free tickets to theme parks. Some timeshare companies will offer you a vacation package at a discounted rate if you come stay at their resort. The discount is often greater if a current owner refers you to the company or resort. Many owners are willing to refer you because they get rewarded by the company if you purchase a timeshare.

Recently, I was able to find an owner in an online forum to refer us to their timeshare company. My wife and I and our four children stayed in a luxurious two bedroom condo right on the beach in southern California. We stayed there for 4 days and 3 nights at a cost of $249. When I went online to check the regular price of our trip, it would have cost us over $1100. We spent about 90 minutes at the timeshare presentation to receive an $851 discount. Our family had a great time and our kids are still talking about how much fun they had at the beach and in the pools.

□

Another way to utilize a timeshare is to find someone willing to rent their timeshare or timeshare points to you. Often if a person is not going to use their timeshare in a given year, they will rent it out to pay for their maintenance fees. My wife and I went to San Diego for 5 days and 4 nights for our 15 year anniversary. I had a friend at work who rented some of her timeshare points to us for only $400. We were able to stay in a luxury condo right by Balboa Park and the Gas Lamp district of San Diego. The cost of a hotel over this particular holiday weekend would have cost us $250-$400 a night just for a room with a bed. Our condo had a full kitchen and we were able to save even more money because we did not have to pay to eat out for every meal.

□

*VRBO.com* (vacation rentals by owner) can be a great way to save when you go on vacation. Often times, you can find a house where you want to go that is cheaper than staying at a hotel or resort. I have a colleague at work who likes to go to Hawaii with her family every summer. She and her husband are able to rent a house for an entire month and they really get to enjoy their time on the island. The total cost of their vacation is drastically cheaper compared to staying at one of the hotels or resorts. Her family is also able to prepare their own food and not have to pay to eat out for every meal. Another benefit is that her kids are able to have their own room.

☐

Disneyland, Disney World, and Disney Cruise Line are often destinations that every family visits or would like to visit. The cost of these vacations have skyrocketed over the last decade. To take my family of 6 to Disneyland/ California Adventure for one day now costs almost $1,000 just for the tickets and parking. That does not include meals or hotel. One way to offset some of the cost of this trip is to get a Chase Disney Visa card. There are usually offers out there where you receive a $100 Disney gift card or statement credit when you sign up for the card. There is occasionally an offer where you receive a $200 Disney gift card for signing up. Chase may also provide a time where you can receive a $50 referral bonus to get other people to sign up for the Disney Credit card. My wife and I signed up at a time Chase was offering a $200 Disney gift card and then later referred our parents to sign up as well. Our parents in turn gave us their gift cards they received when they signed up. We earned $600 in Disney gift cards and reward dollars from our sign up and referral bonuses. Our parents gave us each of their $200 gift cards for a total of $800 more. By doing this, we were able to obtain $1,400 to spend at Disneyland, Disney World, or Disney Cruise line. The other benefit is we receive 1% back in Disney Reward Dollars for every dollar we spent on the credit card. You can also get a Disney credit card that gives you 2% back if you are willing to pay an annual fee.

## 14 EXTRA MONEY

One way to create some room in your budget is to make some extra money. There are numerous ways to do this but I will list a few that my family and I have used over the years to pay off debt and make large purchases.

□

Garage sale: My wife and I usually have a garage sale every spring. We do our spring cleaning and get rid of many of the items we no longer use. We will often tell our friends and family that we are having garage sale in advance. They usually will donate items to us that they want to get rid of as well. We spend a little money to put an ad in the local newspaper and on average we make $200-$300 every time we have a garage sale. Our kids also set up a lemonade and cookie stand at the sale. They usually make $30-$40 selling their items for fifty to seventy five cents each.

☐

Craigslist and eBay: These sites are good tools for making some extra cash. I will usually go through my garage and house to find items I no longer use and there is a demand for. Items that can easily be shipped I often put on eBay and larger items I sell on Craigslist. I recently made $300 selling old video games and video game equipment on eBay. My wife made another $75 selling some old workout DVD's on eBay. EBay has information on its sellers page that can give you ideas of things that are selling well on their site. There is often several thousand dollars worth of stuff around your house that can be sold and you will never miss it. Often times, people do not realize these items are even worth money.

☐

A second job: There are times when it becomes necessary to get a second job to pay the bills, save for something, or cover some unexpected cost. If you are going to be taking more time away from your family, I always recommend maximizing that time. Try to get some sort of job where you can make tips. When my wife and I were first married, she was a waitress and I delivered pizza. We often made more money in tips than we did in our hourly wages. I would make $18-$20 an hour delivering pizza my wife would make double that as a waitress.

## 15 HAVE A PLAN

Now that you have finished this book and have begun to save money every month, the question arises, "What do I do with the extra money?" My answer to that question is have a plan! John L. Beckley said, "Most people don't plan to fail , they fail to plan." During college, I worked in financial services and although I am not a certified financially planner, I would like to share some advice I have learned over the years.

There are four main parts to any solid financial plan and they all combine to equal financial freedom. The four parts are insurance, emergency fund, short term savings and a wealth building/retirement account. These parts fit together much like building a structure.

□

The foundation of the structure is primarily life insurance (income replacement) but also includes your other insurances as well. These insurances are designed to protect your income and savings in the event of a tragedy or misfortune. Without a solid foundation, your financial plan falls apart due to lack of funding when tragedy or misfortune strikes much like a building would collapse without a solid foundation when a storm hits.

☐

The walls of your plan are your emergency fund and short term savings. Both of these components are extremely important because you cannot build wealth when you are going into debt every time there is an emergency or if you have to borrow from your retirement to pay for big life events. These walls support the roof of the structure which is your retirement or wealth building account. If these walls are not sufficiently in place, the roof of the building will collapse. The goal is to always be contributing to the retirement account and never have to borrow from it to meet emergency needs or pay for big life events.

☐

The final part of the structure is the roof which is a retirement or wealth building account. This can be accomplished many ways. It may be an IRA, 401K, 403B, social security, company pension or combination of many things. The goal is to contribute enough money to this account to maintain your current lifestyle or better in retirement.

Every situation is unique and it is wise to outline a detailed financial plan with a certified financial planner. The following is a hypothetical example of what a person could potentially do after reading the Budget Bites book.

In my example, I will assume I am already contributing $250 to savings and/or life insurance and I was able to cut my expenses by $200 a month using some of the ideas in this book giving me a total of $450 dollars to work with each month.

I am the sole provider for my wife and 4 children so I would look to secure a life insurance policy first and foremost. Given that I am in my 30's, I want to lock in a term life policy for 25-30 years. At a super preferred rate I could get $750,000 coverage on myself and $250,000 coverage on my wife for about $85 a month. It is always good to secure a life insurance policy outside of work so that if you lose your job you will not lose your insurance or see your rates skyrocket.

In my scenario, I decided to buy my groceries, gas, and pay for my utilities with a credit card to take advantage of the cash back and discount programs associated with my credit cards. The credit card companies bill me a month later so that I ultimately skipped a month of payments on all the above listed bills. To make sure I have that money in reserve, I would take the $2,500 I did not have to spend for the month and put it into my emergency fund.

I would also utilize some of the ideas out of Chapter 13 (extra money). I would have a garage sale and also sell some items on Craigslist or eBay. I estimate I could earn an additional $500 that would also go into my emergency fund for a total of $3,000.

Ultimately, I would like to have $5,000 in my emergency fund which is the average credit limit on a credit card. $5,000 should cover most emergencies so that I never have to go into debt again when a situation arises. To reach my goal of $5,000, I would set up an automatic draft into my emergency fund account for $65 a month.

The emergency fund contribution combined with my life insurance cost would total $150 a month so far. The remaining $300 of the $450 a month I started with would be split between long term retirement savings and short term savings for college, weddings and the like. I would put $100 of that money toward my short term savings and take advantage of a tax deferred college savings account to save money on my taxes.

The remaining $200 would be put toward retirement and I would once again use a tax deferred vehicle so that I am able to save money on the amount of income tax I have to pay.

My monthly breakdown in this example would look like this:

| | |
|---|---|
| Life Insurance: | $85 |
| Emergency Fund: | $65 |
| Short term Savings: | $100 |
| Retirement: | $200 |
| Total: | $450 |

Although these amounts may not be enough to achieve my goals and dreams, they are definitely a start toward financial freedom. My family would be protected if something were to happen to me or my spouse. I have an emergency fund to draw from if something were to happen to the family car or an appliance. Lastly, I am starting to build wealth for retirement and future family events.

As my income grows and I find other ways to cut my expenses, I can increase these amounts until I reach the numbers that I need to achieve my goals and dreams. There are several financial calculators out there to determine the right numbers for you or you can sit down with a financial planner and he/she could run the numbers for you.

For some people reading this book, debt is the number one factor keeping you from reaching financial freedom and "having a plan." If that is the case, I would recommend looking into one of the many books on debt freedom and making a commitment to resolve this problem no matter the cost. You may also want to sit down with a financial planner who can draw up a plan for your family and hold you accountable when times are tough.

# ABOUT THE AUTHOR

Matthew Johnson is a high school administrator and former mathematics teacher. As a problem solver by nature, he is constantly looking for ways to make his money go further. Matthew and his wife Leah are a single income family raising four children. They have lived and understand many of the financial struggles families face today. After sharing many of his money saving ideas with his friends and family, Matthew saw a need to share them with other families who might be in a similar situation. Budget Bites is Matthew's first book in a series of books designed to help families keep more of their hard earned cash. Matthew obtained his Bachelor of Arts in Business Administration as well as his Master of Arts in Educational Leadership from Azusa Pacific University.

www.ingramcontent.com/pod-product-compliance
Lightning Source LLC
Chambersburg PA
CBHW032307210326
41520CB00047B/2276